Positive Affirmations for Black Women

Increase Self- Confidence and Self- Esteem,
Attract Wealth, Success, Money, Happiness, and
Love

Nia Simone

Contents

Introduction

Never underestimate the power of your mind and your thoughts. Your thoughts are the seeds from which your reality grows. Through thinking, you shape your perceptions, create your narratives, and mold your world. As the saying goes, "You are what you think," and this holds substantial truth in the link between our thoughts, feelings, and actions. Allowing negative thoughts to occupy space in your mind can lead you to believe and internalize them, thereby damaging your sense of self. However, keeping positive thoughts in your mind can uplift, energize, and create a reality infused with optimism and opportunity! You will internalize this positive energy and feel better by keeping positive thoughts in your mind. You have the power to manifest a brighter future for yourself because your thoughts influence your world. When you consciously direct your thoughts toward what you desire, you put energy into bringing your aspirations to life. Positive thinking can be very potent.

Positive affirmations are an excellent tool in this transformative process. They are statements we repeat to ourselves, aiming to shift our mindset and foster positive thinking patterns. These affirmations can become automatic responses with repetition and belief, essentially rewiring our brains for positivity and success. When you consistently replace negative self-talk with positive affirmations, you gradually alter your thought patterns, promoting a healthier self-image, improved well-being, and a more confident approach toward life. In this way, the cycle of our thoughts, affirmations, actions, and realities becomes a self-fulfilling prophecy – you truly start to become what you think.

I encourage you to say each affirmation aloud and to own its power. You may also repeat the affirmation in your mind, write it down on paper, or type it on your computer. Try to read these affirmations and repeat them as often as possible. The more you hear and repeat them, the more your mind will absorb them. I find reading these affirmations in the morning and before going to bed puts me in a very healthy and positive headspace. I wish the same for you.

Affirmations

I embrace my blackness as a source of comfort, strength, and pride.

My beauty radiates from the inside out, and it is powerful.

I am a light of hope, strength, determination, and wisdom, inspiring those around me.

I deserve success, and every day I work towards accomplishing my dreams.

My life is a testament to the power of perseverance and resilience.

I honor the legacy of the strong black women who came before me and continue their fight for equality.

Every hurdle I overcome strengthens my spirit and determination.

I set my expectations high.

I am God's masterpiece.

My natural hair is a crown, which I wear with confidence and pride.

I am unapologetically black and a woman, and I celebrate both daily.

I trust in my ability to rise above any challenge that comes my way.

I am worthy of respect, love, and kindness.

I will never give up or be brought down. I will always rise up and move forward.

I am resourceful and capable; there is nothing I cannot do.

I am resilient, and I never give up.

I am a black queen, comfortable in my skin and confident in my power.

The universe favors me, and I always attract positivity and abundance.

My voice matters, my opinion counts, and I am heard.

I make time for myself every day because I am important.

I can change my narrative and rewrite my story anytime I choose.

I am a strong and confident black woman.

I am a creator of change, an innovator of ideas, and a warrior for justice.

I set my expectations high and accept nothing less.

I am stronger than you think, do not underestimate me.

I am blessed with the spirit of my ancestors, and their wisdom guides me.

I love what I see in the mirror; I look good today and every day.

My skin is beautiful and radiant.

I am attracting wealth and health.

My journey may be challenging, but it is shaping me into an even stronger, more resilient black woman.

Each dollar I spend will return abundantly and build my wealth.

My value is determined by me, not by other people.

I breathe in certainty and breathe out uncertainty.

I am determined to become prosperous.

When I fall down, I get up with grace and purpose.

I am bringing success, wealth, independence, and prosperity into my life.

I honor and am grateful for the balance between my career and my family.

I am worthy of love and respect.

I am enough. I am an empowered black woman.

I am beautifully imperfect.

I am allowed to be myself and show people who I am.

I attract genuine friendships with people who want the best for me.

I am a capable black woman; I can overcome any obstacle.

I am fierce, and I am loyal, and I am determined.

The love I have for myself increases my capacity to love others.

I am confident in all of my endeavors.

My feelings are valid and should be honored.

I honor my strength and celebrate my unique journey as a black woman.

Every day, I am unfolding into the best version of myself.

I am limitless in my potential and boundless in my worth.

I radiate beauty, intelligence, and grace that is uniquely my own.

I am a powerhouse; I am indestructible.

My skin is a testament to resilience, my spirit a testament to strength.

My voice matters, my ideas are valuable, and my actions are powerful.

I am a beacon of light and a pillar of strength to those around me.

The love I have for myself is a reflection of my strength and inner beauty.

I deserve all the love, joy, and opportunities the world has to offer.

I embrace my heritage, my journey, and my future with open arms.

I am a queen who rules my world with love, wisdom, and courage.

Every challenge I face is an opportunity to grow and assert my strength.

I am worthy of respect, love, and fulfillment.

My power lies in my ability to face adversity with courage and grace.

I am a constant work of art, perpetually evolving and eternally beautiful.

I am enough just as I am.

I am equipped to succeed.

I acknowledge my worth and stand tall in my power.

My dreams are valid, my goals are achievable, and my vision is clear.

My journey is a testament to my strength and resilience as a black woman.

I am my ancestors' greatest dreams, forging a path for future generations.

I am a representation of strength, resilience, and beauty.

I am proud of the woman I am and the woman I am becoming.

I manifest joy, success, and love into my life every single day.

My potential is unlimited, and my future is bright.

I am gentle with myself and show myself kindness and compassion.

I keep my mind filled with positive, uplifting thoughts and release any negative thoughts.

I belong in any space I walk into.

I am capable, intelligent, and deserving of success and happiness.

I love and accept myself fully, flaws and all.

My beauty is precious and unique and cannot be defined by external standards.

I am powerful and resilient and can overcome any obstacle.

I honor and celebrate my cultural heritage and identity.

I trust myself to make the best decisions for my life and well-being.

I am worthy of forgiveness and grace both from others and myself.

I am confident and capable and can achieve anything I want.

I am a supportive network that encourages and motivates me.

I have faith in my decisions and actions.

I am creating a network of strong, like-minded women to support me.

With my positive mindset, I attract success easily and effortlessly to me.

I can make my own path.

I won't let anyone look down upon me.

A greater force won't silence me.

I embrace leaving my comfort zone; even though it can be daunting, it is where my growth takes place.

I can conquer anything if I want.

I embrace the greatness within me.

I am proud of my cultural heritage.

I am comfortable in setting boundaries and sticking with them.

The love I have for myself increases my capacity to love others.

I focus on what gives me energy. My energy serves as my compass.

I am a woman of value, and I expect others to treat me as such.

I deserve everything I want.

I conquer all obstacles by knowing I am capable.

I have control of my destiny and find peace in this.

I see the big picture and will not be discouraged by small problems.

I have everything I need and more.

I am my best source of inspiration.

I am one step closer to reaching my goal when I fail at something.

I am unconditionally worthy of living my best life and attaining all my goals.

I am a black woman, beautifully crafted, divinely inspired, and deserving of all good things.

I am blessed, and I am loved.

My heart knows joy, and my soul knows peace.

When others go low, I go high.

I am more than I was yesterday and always getting better.

I am a resourceful, proud, and powerful black woman.

Regardless of the outcome, I am supported, loved, and respected.

I am stepping into my power with style and confidence.

I am courageous; I do not back down.

I am blessed with unique talents.

I am creative.

I am in charge of and proud of my body.

I deserve to be where I am.

There is power in my thought.

I have a positive mindset and move forward with grace.

My possibilities are endless; I can and will have it all.

I am fierce and can be a warrior when I need to be.

My mind is powerful and focused on achieving all of my dreams.

I work hard, I love hard, and I am the best there is.

I command respect and will accept nothing less.

I am successful and capable of solving any problem.

I strive to learn something new each and every day.

I can handle anything that comes my way.

I prioritize my commitment to be good to myself.

I practice having compassion for myself.

I like to have fun and play; they are necessary and good for my soul.

I love fully, with passion, and with my whole heart.

♥

Allowing myself to rest and recover is part of taking care of myself.

♥

By doing less, I can receive more.

♥

I soar above others who seek to bring me down.

♥

When I get overwhelmed, I breathe and slow my thoughts.

♥

I look in the mirror and see a dynamic, powerful, radiant woman.

♥

I do not need a man.

♥

I prioritize my peace and always seek balance in my life.

♥

I draw strength from history.

I am committed to becoming my best self.

Each dollar I spend will return abundantly.

I breathe in certainty and breathe out uncertainty.

I am focused on my prosperity.

I am pulling wealth and prosperity into my life.

I am worthy of love and respect.

Who I am is enough.

I am beautifully imperfect.

I am allowed to be myself and show people who I am.

I attract genuine friendships with people who want the best for me.

The love I have for myself increases my capacity to love others.

I belong in any space I walk into.

I am my best source of inspiration.

I am unconditionally worthy.

Regardless of the outcome, I am supported.

I am stepping into my power.

I am blessed with unique talents.

I am creative.

I am smart.

I deserve to be where I am.

I embrace learning something new every day. I embrace my blackness; it is a source of strength and pride.

My beauty radiates from the inside out and cannot be contained or defined by society's standards.

I am a beacon of hope and wisdom, inspiring those around me.

I place a crown upon my head because I am a queen.

I deserve success, and every day I work toward my dreams.

My life is a testament to the power of perseverance and resilience.

I honor the legacy of the strong black women who came before me and continue their fight for equality.

Every hurdle I overcome strengthens my spirit and determination.

My natural hair is a crown, which I wear with confidence and pride.

I am unapologetically black and a woman, and I celebrate both daily.

I trust in my ability to rise above any challenge that comes my way.

I am worthy of love, respect, and kindness. Others do not determine my value.

♥

I am a black queen, comfortable in my skin and confident in my power.

♥

The universe conspires in my favor, and I attract positivity and abundance.

♥

My voice matters, my opinion counts, and I am heard.

♥

I have the power to change my narrative and rewrite my story.

♥

I am a creator of change, an innovator of ideas, and a warrior for justice.

♥

My melanin is magical. It embodies my strength, heritage, and resilience.

♥

I am blessed with the spirit of my ancestors, and their wisdom guides me.

♥

I am a black woman, beautifully crafted, divinely inspired, and deserving of all good things.

My journey may be challenging, but it is shaping me into an even stronger, more resilient black woman.

I use intrinsic power to improve myself and those around me.

I am focused on my path to success and happiness.

I bring my magic and spark to absolutely everything I do.

I am beautifully unique and embrace my individuality.

Each dollar I spend returns to me abundantly; I am financially prosperous.

I breathe in confidence and breathe out uncertainty.

I am attracting wealth and prosperity into my life.

I am worthy of love, respect, and kindness.

My imperfections contribute to my beautiful individuality.

Self-care is not an indulgence; it's a necessity for my well-being.

I am allowed to be myself and show the world my true identity.

I attract genuine friendships with people who want the best for me.

The love I have for myself increases my capacity to love others.

By shining my light, I help others shine theirs.

I belong in any space I walk into; my presence is valuable.

Being me is my superpower; it's how I win.

My self-worth is high; I am invaluable.

My feelings are valid, and I honor them all.

I am stepping into my power; I am unstoppable.

I am blessed with unique talents and skills that I use to make a difference.

I am creative, and my ideas are valuable.

I deserve to be where I am and have earned my achievements.

I embrace learning something new daily; it's a path to growth.

I am capable of everything I desire.

There is room for me in any space I choose to occupy.

I am a symbol of strength and power.

If I can, I can. I am in control of my destiny.

I am an artist, and the world is my canvas.

I am worthy of success and work hard to achieve my dreams.

I am a creator; I bring unique ideas to life.

I am smart; my intelligence is a tool for success.

I am an entrepreneur; I am a pioneer of change.

I am a black woman, and I am proud of my identity.

I am capable, intelligent, and deserving of success and happiness.

I love and accept myself fully, flaws and all.

My beauty is unique and valuable and cannot be defined by external standards.

I am deserving of self-care and prioritizing my own needs and well-being.

I am powerful and resilient and can overcome any obstacle.

I trust myself to make the best decisions for my life and well-being.

♥

I deserve to have healthy and fulfilling relationships that uplift and support me.

♥

I honor and celebrate my cultural heritage and identity.

♥

I am enough, just as I am. I do not need to strive for perfection.

♥

I deserve to set boundaries and assert myself in all areas of my life.

♥

My voice and perspective are valuable and worthy of being heard.

♥

I am worthy of forgiveness and grace both from others and myself.

♥

I am confident and capable and can achieve anything I want.

♥

I am allowed to be myself and show people who I am.

The love I have for myself increases my capacity to love others.

I dare to confront anything that doesn't feel right for me.

Courage is with me every moment of every day, no matter what may come my way.

By shining my light, I help others shine theirs.

I belong in any space I walk into.

Being me is how I win.

I am a beautiful, powerful black woman, and my strength knows no limits.

I honor the richness of my heritage and draw strength from it daily.

I am a bold leader, making a difference in this world.

I am deserving of success and all good things in life.

I embrace my unique black beauty, inside and out.

I am a queen and will not let anyone treat me with disrespect.

I am a ray of light, shining my brilliance wherever I go.

I am perfect, embodying the strength of my ancestors.

I am intelligent and capable; my potential is limitless.

I am proud of my skin, hair, culture, and everything that makes me a Black woman.

I rise above any challenges and adversity I face.

My body is perfect the way it is.

I love and appreciate myself and all the journeys that have brought me here.

I am a vessel of creativity, bursting with ideas and innovation.

I am confident and unstoppable in the pursuit of my dreams.

I am worthy of respect, love, and kindness, just as I am.

I am a black woman, and that alone makes me extraordinary.

I am constantly growing, learning, and evolving.

I am a role model, inspiring those around me with my actions.

I am enough, exactly as I am, and I do not need to prove myself to anyone.

I celebrate my big and small victories as they contribute to my journey.

I am compassionate and kind, spreading love wherever I go.

Stereotypes do not define me; I am uniquely me.

I let go of self-doubt, and I embrace self-confidence.

I am a warrior, unafraid to fight for what I believe in.

I am an agent of change, using my voice for the betterment of my community.

I am deeply loved and cherished by those around me.

I am a woman of substance, leaving my mark wherever I go.

I am powerful beyond measure, unafraid to wield my influence.

I am a black woman, proud, strong, and unapologetically me.

I am blessed with unique talents.

I am creative, smart, and fully deserving of my achievements.

Every day, I embrace the opportunity to learn and grow.

I am capable of accomplishing any idea I conceive.

I walk into every room as if I belong because I do.

Success, health, and joy are my birthrights.

The strength I need is within me.

I am allowed to be myself and show people who I am.

I am loved and lovable; anyone who does not see that is not worth my time.

I attract genuine friendships with people who want the best for me.

I create space for people to show up for me and support me.

The love I have for myself increases my capacity to love others.

I don't have to earn my worth; I am inherently worthy.

I focus on what gives me energy. My energy serves as my compass.

Being me is my greatest strength.

I am my best source of inspiration.

I honor and validate all my feelings.

I allow myself to feel so I can heal.

I am stepping into my power.

I inhale my courage and exhale my fears.

I turn my dreams into goals and my goals into reality.

My success is inevitable, for I am determined and resilient.

I am more than capable of overcoming the challenges I face.

I choose to rise above negativity and embrace positivity.

I am carving out my path to success, one step at a time.

I can do anything I set my mind to.

I will not settle for anything less than I deserve.

I am worthy of wealth and abundance.

The wealth I seek is also seeking me.

I am a magnet for financial opportunities and prosperity.

My unique talents and skills bring me wealth and success.

Every day I am moving closer to my financial goals.

I attract money and wealth effortlessly into my life.

My actions create constant prosperity.

I am open and receptive to all the wealth life brings me.

Money flows freely and abundantly into my life.

My wealth shines from within me.

I deserve to be financially successful and secure.

I am grateful for the wealth that is in my life.

My positive relationship with money grows every day.

I am capable and able to create wealth and success.

I am financially abundant, and money comes to me naturally.

With my positive attitude, I attract abundance to my life.

I am grateful for the strong women who came before me.

My mind is attuned to creating wealth.

I have a wealth mindset.

I am in control of my financial future.

I am creating a life of abundance and prosperity.

I am successful in my financial endeavors.

My income is constantly increasing.

I set my intention to attract wealth and financial success.

I do not waste my time with people who want to bring me down.

I have a great relationship with money: it loves me, and I love it.

Wealth and success are normal for me.

I am beautifully imperfect and proud of it.

Who I am is enough, and I deserve all great things.

Every space I walk into is better because of my presence.

I am an embodiment of strength and resilience.

I am loved, respected, and cherished.

I am stepping into my power, leaving no room for self-doubt.

♥

My potential to succeed is limitless.

♥

My skin is radiant; my spirit is vibrant; I am beautiful.

♥

My life is filled with joy, prosperity, and fulfillment.

♥

The love I have for myself increases my capacity to love others.

♥

I belong in any space I walk into; my presence matters.

♥

I am headed in the right direction.

♥

My worth is inherent and does not need to be earned.

♥

I am confident in my abilities and intelligence.

My feelings are valid, and I honor them all.

I am my best source of inspiration.

Being me is my biggest advantage.

I celebrate the uniqueness of my journey, embracing every experience as an opportunity for growth.

I am gentle with myself through all transitions.

My talents are unique, and they open doors for me.

My voice is powerful, and my thoughts are valid.

I can achieve any goal I set for myself.

I am a creator, capable of bringing my visions to life.

I am smart and deserving of all the opportunities I seek.

I embrace learning something new every day.

I attract genuine friendships with people who want the best for me.

I am a force of positivity, radiating light and love.

Every challenge I face is an opportunity for me to demonstrate my strength.

My energy serves as my compass, guiding me toward my true purpose.

I am unapologetically myself, and I love who I am.

Others' opinions do not define my worth.

I am a warrior, ready to conquer any obstacles in my path.

I am blessed with an abundance of opportunities and success.

My self-worth is high, and no one can take it away.

I am positive, and I hold my head high.

I am power, grace, strength, courage, and wisdom.

I have so much to look forward to; I am grateful for having such a wonderful life with endless possibilities.

Every day, in every way, I am becoming more confident in my abilities.

I am blessed with an abundance of talent which I will use to better the world.

I recognize my inherent worth and will not let anyone undermine it.

My journey is unique, and every experience propels me towards success.

I will only give up once I have tried absolutely everything.

I believe in myself, and I believe in the path I have chosen.

I do not compare myself to anyone else.

I am destined to accomplish greatness.

I breathe in and surround myself with positivity.

I am rooted in my culture, giving me a powerful identity.

I embrace my melanin skin, which is as beautiful as it is strong.

My words, thoughts, and opinions matter.

I am a warrior and a queen, fully equipped to conquer life's battles.

I am an emblem of beauty, grace, and resilience.

My imperfections make me unique and contribute to my beauty.

I know and accept that I am connected to something greater than myself.

I am more than enough, just the way I am.

Every day I am growing and becoming a better version of myself.

I embrace my natural hair; it is a crown of glory.

I surround myself with love and positivity.

I respect myself and command respect from others.

I am powerful beyond measure.

I exude confidence, charisma, and charm.

I am deserving of success, prosperity, and happiness.

My voice is a potent tool for change, and I will use it.

I am a masterpiece sculpted to perfection.

I am a trailblazer, a leader, and an influencer.

I celebrate my heritage; it is the fabric of my being.

The chaos around me is no match for the calmness within me.

I am at peace with who I am and my journey.

I am a unique embodiment of love, strength, and resilience.

My peace is my power, and I will not allow anyone or anything to disturb it.

I am secure and at ease in my skin, celebrating its radiant beauty daily.

As I nourish my spirit, I cultivate an inner peace that empowers me.

I trust in the divine timing of my life, releasing all stress and anxiety.

My mind is a sanctuary of tranquility, and I guard it fiercely.

Each breath fills me with peace, and each exhalation releases my worries.

I am a beacon of tranquility amidst life's storms, grounded in my worth and identity.

I vibrate at the frequency of peace, attracting serenity in all aspects of my life.

The peace I hold within me radiates, creating harmonious spaces around me.

My journey, filled with ups and downs, contributes to my peace as I embrace each moment.

I deserve peace, joy, and love in all their forms.

I stand tall, knowing my ancestors and their wisdom guide me.

My peace is my strength, and I cultivate it every day.

I am a divine being of calm and serenity; my peace is a testament to my strength.

In every situation, I respond with grace, patience, and tranquility.

I am a well of tranquility; my calm influences the world around me.

Peace is my birthright; I claim it daily in thought, word, and action.

My peace is a powerful shield, protecting me from negativity and harm.

I am serene in a chaotic world, easily maintaining my equilibrium.

My inner peace is a fortress, allowing me to navigate life's storms gracefully.

I am more than my struggles; I am a woman of peace and strength.

I bask in the tranquility of my inner world, drawing strength and courage from it.

I am at peace, knowing I am doing my best and moving forward.

I am a creator, capable of birthing dreams into reality.

Stereotypes or societal norms will not limit me; I am boundless.

I am a beacon of love and compassion; I attract the same.

My heart is open, ready to receive the love I desire.

I am deserving of a love that is pure, honest, and deep.

I attract love effortlessly in my life because I am worthy of love.

I am a strong, beautiful black woman worthy of being loved fully and completely.

I draw love and romance into my life with ease and grace.

My love story is filled with passion, respect, and mutual understanding.

My melanin is radiant, and it attracts love and light.

I am blessed with an abundance of love from others.

My inner beauty naturally attracts the right people into my life.

I love myself unconditionally and, in doing so, attract others who love me in the same way.

I am deserving of a love as strong and empowering as I am.

I am a queen who attracts a partner who values my worth.

I am open to giving and receiving love in its purest form.

I attract relationships that uplift me and enhance my growth.

Every relationship I enter is enriching and filled with love.

I am attracting a partner who respects me and cherishes our relationship.

I am empowered, valued, and loved.

I am aligned with the energy of love and abundance.

I am unstoppable.

My unique qualities make me attractive and lovable.

I am attracting my soulmate toward me at this very moment.

I give love freely, and it is returned to me multiplied.

I am open, ready, and deserving of a loving, healthy relationship.

I am attracting love and positive energy into my life.

I am a magnet for love and prosperity in all aspects of my life.

I believe in myself. I am here for a reason.

Happiness is always around me; I only need to open my heart and eyes.

I have the power to change the way I am feeling by changing my perspective.

I am ready to give and receive true love.

I am blessed with curiosity and inquisitiveness.

I am a role model for all to behold.

Every day I start fresh and move forward.

I am beautifully and wonderfully made, with unique strengths and abilities.

I am confident in my own skin and my own abilities.

I deserve to occupy spaces with grace, power, and authority.

I am resilient, strong, and capable of facing any challenge that comes my way.

I embrace my individuality and uniqueness unapologetically.

I am the definition of a strong, intelligent, beautiful, resilient, and courageous black woman.

Society's expectations and standards do not define me.

I will always be treated with love, respect, and dignity.

My beauty extends beyond my physical appearance; it radiates from within.

I am extremely proud of my family, our accomplishments, our heritage, and our culture.

My voice matters, and my opinions are valuable.

I deserve all the good that life has to offer.

I am a source of inspiration to those around me.

I celebrate my triumphs and learn from my failures.

I choose to love and accept myself just as I am.

I honor my body, my mind, and my spirit.

I am deserving of love, joy, and prosperity.

I am a powerful creator, capable of manifesting my dreams and aspirations.

My journey, with its triumphs and struggles, makes me who I am.

I release any negative thoughts about myself and embrace positive self-talk.

I choose to shine my light and not hide my greatness.

I am at peace with who I am, who I am, and who I will become.

I am worthy of success, and I claim it.

I bring value and make a significant impact in my chosen field.

I can change my narrative and direct my life's course.

I deserve justice and respect and will not settle for less.

I listen to my body when it needs rest; I rest.

I choose to practice gratitude and see all the many things I am thankful for.

I am a strong, determined, resourceful, and capable person.

I have done difficult things in the past, and I can and will do them again.

I am allowed to feel my feelings, all of them.

I am allowed to be upset, angry, and sad sometimes.

My boundaries are important, and I honor them so that other people will.

I am capable of accomplishing my goals and reaping their rewards.

I am wise and calm and a source of strength to those around me.

My worth is not dependent on other's opinions of me.

I am a source of power and inspiration to others.

I am valuable and deserving of every opportunity and blessing.

I trust in my capabilities and believe in my potential.

I bring light and joy into the world.

I am in charge of words, my actions, my reactions, and my life.

I am in control of my destiny. If I can envision it, I can make it happen.

I do the right thing, and I do it very well.

I take strength in my ability to overcome and conquer.

I am an example of power, love, and resilience.

My skin is beautiful, my voice is powerful, and my spirit is unbreakable.

I embrace and celebrate the beauty of my natural hair and radiant skin.

I am worthy of love, respect, and all the world's happiness.

I am enough, just as I am, and I do not need to change for anyone.

My flaws make me unique and beautiful; they are part of my strength.

I am a vibrant, valuable, and respected member of my community.

Society's stereotypes do not define me; I express myself.

I am a magnet for positive energy and profitable opportunities.

I believe in my potential, and every day, I am achieving great things.

My ancestors' strength and courage run through my veins, fueling my determination.

I am deserving of wealth, prosperity, and a life of abundance.

Every dollar I spend, I spend wisely.

♥

I am in harmony with my success; I easily create and seize opportunities.

♥

The passion of my dreams fuels me, and I pave the way for others.

♥

My melanin is a testament to my strength and beauty. I celebrate my heritage every day.

♥

I am the embodiment of grace, courage, and wisdom.

♥

I am powerful beyond measure. I rise above any challenge.

♥

My creativity shines bright, illuminating my path to success.

♥

I honor my journey and recognize my growth. I am proud of who I am becoming.

♥

My intuition and wisdom guide every decision I make.

I embody unyielding courage, moving through life with confidence and determination.

My voice is powerful, and my words inspire and uplift others.

I do the hard things that others cannot do.

I am a trendsetter, leading with my creativity and innovation.

I am a powerful force, radiating positive energy in all I do.

I celebrate my big and small victories and am grateful for my journey.

I am a thriving entrepreneur, turning my vision into reality with confidence and determination.

I am a role model, inspiring the next generation with strength and resilience.

I embrace my roots, celebrate my culture, and honor my heritage. They are the backbone of my strength.

I am in charge of my destiny. I move closer to my goals with each passing day.

I am a symbol of success, perseverance, and strength.

I walk in my purpose with conviction and courage. My passion illuminates my path.

Others do not define my worth; I define my success.

My talent and hard work pave the way for my success. I am proud of my accomplishments.

Every setback is an opportunity for an even greater comeback. I rise with strength and grace.

I inspire others with my wisdom, strength, resilience, and perseverance.

My black is beautiful, my spirit is indomitable, and my potential is limitless.

I lead by example and rise above my troubles.

I love who I am and am proud of the woman I am becoming.

I am blessed with a mind eager to learn and a heart ready to love.

My journey is unique and important, and I trust my path.

My ideas are valuable, and my creative potential is limitless.

I can handle anything that comes my way with grace and confidence.

I am rooted in my culture and connected to my history; both give me a sense of identity and strength.

The love I have for myself amplifies the love I give to others.

I am deserving of a fulfilling and prosperous life.

I attract genuine friendships with people who respect and value me.

I am a dynamic, influential woman who is capable of achieving anything.

My success is inevitable; every step I take is a step toward my goals.

I am focused on my health, my happiness, and my future.

My confidence shines through in everything I do.

I am comfortable in my skin, and I shine with the brilliance of self-love.

I use my voice for good, a powerful instrument for change.

I am fully in charge of my future. I decide my paI am the only one who can dictate the outcome.

I am safe, and I am well.

I am healthy, and I am loved.

I surround myself with love and positivity in all areas of my life.

I feel gratitude for the abundant blessings in my life.

I am confident in my ability to make wise decisions.

I am resilient, and I bounce back stronger from every setback.

I respect myself and my boundaries, and I know my worth.

Every room I walk into is better because I am there.

My joy, peace, and happiness are priorities, and I protect them.

I deserve respect, and I expect to be treated with respect.

My intelligence and creativity open doors for me.

I am worthy of success, love, and complete happiness.

I am manifesting my dreams into reality with every step I take.

I am proud of my heritage and roots; they make me who I am.

I am powerful beyond measure, and my influence is significant.

My presence is a gift to the world, and I am appreciated.

I trust myself and trust in the journey that I'm on.

I have the power to create the life that I desire.

I am loved, appreciated, and respected in all.

I am a beacon of strength, love, and resilience.

My skin is beautiful, my voice is powerful, and my spirit is unbreakable.

♥

I embrace and celebrate the beauty of my natural hair and radiant skin.

♥

I am worthy of love, respect, and all the world's happiness.

♥

I am enough, just as I am, and I do not need to change for anyone.

♥

My flaws make me unique and beautiful; they are part of my strength.

♥

I am a vibrant, valuable, and respected member of my community.

♥

Society's stereotypes do not define me; I express myself.

♥

I am a magnet for positive energy and ample opportunities.

♥

I believe in my potential, and every day, I am achieving great things.

I choose my friends carefully and do not let others bring me down.

My ancestors' strength and courage run through my veins, fueling my determination.

I am deserving of wealth, prosperity, and happiness.

Every decision I make is a step toward fulfilling my personal growth and development mission.

I love who I am and am proud of the woman I am becoming.

I am blessed with a mind eager to learn and a heart ready to love.

My journey is unique and important, and I trust my path.

My ideas are valuable, and my creative potential is limitless.

I can handle anything that comes my way with grace and confidence.

I am rooted in my culture and connected to my history; both give me a sense of identity and strength.

I show myself kindness and compassion.

The love I have for myself amplifies the love I give to others.

I am deserving of a fulfilling and prosperous life.

I attract genuine friendships with people who respect and value me.

I am a dynamic, influential woman who is capable of achieving anything.

My success is inevitable; every step I take is a step toward my goals.

I am focused on my health, my happiness, and my future.

I surround myself with people who love and care for me.

My confidence shines through in everything I do.

I am comfortable in my skin, and I shine with the brilliance of self-love.

I use my voice for good, a powerful instrument for change.

I surround myself with people who honor me.

I am grateful and thankful for the abundant blessings in my life.

I am confident in my ability to make wise decisions.

I am resilient, and I bounce back stronger from every setback.

I respect myself and my boundaries, and I know my worth.

Every room I walk into is better because I am there.

My joy, peace, and happiness are priorities, and I protect them.

I am deserving of respect, and I accept nothing less.

My intelligence and creativity open doors for me.

I am worthy of success, love, and complete happiness.

I am manifesting my dreams into reality with every step I take.

I am proud of my heritage and roots; they make me who I am.

I am powerful beyond measure, and my influence is significant.

My presence is a gift to the world, and I am appreciated.

I trust myself and trust in the journey that I'm on.

I have the power to create the life that I desire.

I am loved, appreciated, and respected.

I do not accept less than I deserve.

I am blessed with unique talents, and I embrace them wholeheartedly.

I am a creative force, using my creativity to shape the world.

I am smart and capable of achieving great things in all aspects of my life.

I deserve to be where I am today and have earned my success.

I embrace learning something new daily, and this growth empowers me.

I can accomplish any idea I think of, as I hold the power to manifest my dreams.

My love for myself increases my capacity to love and accept others.

I am always headed in the right direction, even when the path is unclear.

I don't have to earn my worth; it is inherent.

I belong in any space I walk into and own it with grace and confidence.

I focus on what gives me energy, and this serves as my compass in life.

Being myself is my greatest strength and how I win in life.

I am my best source of inspiration, drawing on my experiences and wisdom.

My self-worth is high, unaffected by external influences or opinions.

I am the best version of myself, just as I am, and I cherish my unique identity.

I find new ways to come home to myself each day, nurturing my relationship with myself.

I am unconditionally worthy of love, success, and happiness.

I am gentle with myself through all transitions, understanding that change is a part of growth.

Regardless of the outcome, I am supported and loved.

My feelings are valid, and I honor them in all their complexity.

I allow myself to feel so I can heal, recognizing the power of emotional wellness.

My magic speaks for itself, as I am a powerful and inspiring woman.

I am stepping into my power, embracing the strength that lies within me.

I inhale confidence and exhale doubts, filling myself with self-belief and positive energy.

I see self-worth and know it.

I celebrate the strength and resilience that lies within my heritage.

I am a queen, creating my unique path to greatness.

My blackness is a gift, not a burden.

I embody the beauty and spirit of my ancestors.

I am a vibrant, powerful woman of color.

My skin is an incredible testament to resilience and beauty.

I am enough, exactly as I am.

I trust in the power of my dreams and passions.

♥

I surround myself with love, support, and positive energy.

♥

My success and happiness are inevitable.

♥

I am more than enough, and I get better every day.

♥

I am worthy of all the respect and love that comes my way.

♥

I radiate beauty, charm, and grace.

♥

My voice matters, and my thoughts are valuable.

♥

I am proud of who I am, and I embrace my power.

♥

I am making a significant difference in the world.

My spirit is beautiful, and my mind is strong.

I am a fearless achiever, and my potential is limitless.

I am deserving of all the blessings coming my way.

I am a representation of grace, courage, and wisdom.

My actions inspire others to dream more and become more.

Every day, I am learning and growing into a better me.

I embrace my unique journey and celebrate my progress.

I am a dynamic, irreplaceable woman of substance.

I am capable of achieving all my dreams and desires.

I embrace my uniqueness and the beauty it brings to the world.

My melanin is radiant, strong, and beautiful.

I am creating the life I deserve and have the power to make it happen.

I am capable of greatness and will not let any obstacles deter me.

My blackness is a strength, not a weakness.

I deserve success, happiness, and love in all forms.

I cannot control other people's behavior, but I can and will control how I react.

My intelligence is an invaluable asset that propels me forward.

My voice matters, and I will not be silenced.

I am more than a survivor; I am a warrior.

I am confident in my abilities and will continue to grow and learn.

I am a beacon of resilience and perseverance.

I am proud of who I am and where I come from.

I am a source of inspiration for myself and others.

I will not let anyone define me; I am the author of my own story.

My beauty transcends societal standards.

My potential is limitless, and I am full of possibilities.

I am deserving of respect and will not settle for less.

I will let go of fear and embrace new opportunities.

My strength is in my authenticity and honesty.

I am powerful, and my impact is significant.

I am in charge of my fate and the captain of my soul.

I am worthy of all the good that is coming my way.

My contributions are valuable and make a difference.

Others' opinions of me do not determine my self-worth.

I am proud of my black heritage; it inspires me to strive for greatness.

I come from a proud and amazing family.

I surround myself with people who love and support me.

My roots are strong, and my future is limitless.

I see myself as the powerful, awe-inspiring, capable black woman I am.

I am an embodiment of resilience, grace, and power.

Every hue of my skin is a testament to my unique beauty and strength.

I embrace the wisdom and strength inherited from the queens before me.

I possess the courage to thrive in any circumstance.

My spirit is invincible, a symbol of divine power.

I find my pride and purpose in the rich tapestry of my heritage.

I am a beacon of light, igniting change and empowerment.

My voice matters, my story is significant, and my existence is impactful.

I am the sculptor of my destiny, molding dreams into reality.

My potential is boundless, and my accomplishments are remarkable.

I am vibrant, upbeat, and victorious.

The echoes of my ancestors' strength and perseverance guide my journey.

In every stride, I am redefining history and leaving a legacy.

My natural beauty is an undeniable declaration of self-love.

In my eyes sparkles the strength of a thousand suns.

I am nurturing, compassionate, and a symbol of unfathomable love.

Obstacles only make me stronger and wiser.

♥

Like my spirit, my hair is uncontainable and a symbol of freedom.

♥

I am a canvas of possibility, painting my life with strokes of triumph.

♥

My worth isn't defined by other people's beliefs but by my self-love.

♥

Every inch of me radiates with purpose, passion, and power.

♥

I am a queen, reigning in the kingdom of self-assured confidence.

♥

My mind is an arsenal of creativity and innovation.

♥

The rhythm of my heart harmonizes with the song of success.

♥

The reflection in my mirror is an emblem of extraordinary strength, beauty, and intelligence.

My creativity and skills are my wealth; I leverage them to build a prosperous future.

I am my best advocate, valuing my talents and worth in the business world.

My skin color is not a barrier but a badge of pride and strength that fuels my journey to success.

I am comfortable in my skin and proud of my heritage, which propels me to reach greater heights in my career.

My voice matters in business, and my input brings unique value and perspective.

I deserve abundance, financial freedom, and wealth. I welcome these blessings into my life.

I can handle the challenges that come my way in business and use them to grow and prosper.

I am building a legacy of success and wealth for myself and my community.

Every step in my career path is a step towards realizing my dreams.

My mindset towards money is positive; I believe in my ability to attain wealth.

As a black woman, I am a symbol of strength, perseverance, and resilience in business.

I am paving the way for other black women in business, demonstrating that success and wealth are possible for us.

I nurture and utilize my unique talents to create business success and generate wealth.

I embrace my ability to adapt, innovate, and thrive, ensuring my financial abundance.

I harness the power of positivity to overcome hurdles on my path to financial success.

I am creating a thriving business built on my unique vision and fortified by my unmatched dedication.

Every business success I achieve is proof of my capabilities and a step closer to my financial goals.

I am a role model, inspiring other black women to reach for their dreams and achieve business success.

The wealth I am attracting enriches my life and positively impacts those around me.

I am building a prosperous future based on my values, intelligence, and the richness of my culture.

I reject any limitations put upon me. My potential is boundless, and my success is inevitable.

In my journey towards wealth, I remain true to myself, honoring my roots and experiences as a black woman.

My business ventures are successful, bringing prosperity and positive change into my life.

I radiate confidence and determination, drawing opportunities and wealth toward me.

As a black woman, I write a story of success, empowerment, and wealth for myself and future generations.

I am a magnet for financial success and prosperity.

Every dollar I make amplifies my impact and influences positive change.

I deserve to be financially secure and successful.

My financial growth is an extension of my self-worth and capability. I choose my friends carefully. I embrace and hold close my friends who love me.

I recognize the true people in my life and let them go.

I surround myself with friends who support and love me and want the absolute best for me. I have no time for the haters.

Every hardship I go through will make me better for the future. These hardships are tools that make me stronger.

My family is a source of strength to me. Some of my family are related to me by blood, others are not, and they all have my back.

I will always trust myself to make the best decision for myself.

I listen to my mind and allow my wisdom to direct me down the right path.

I love my friends and family, even if they do not understand the decisions I make or the directions I take.

I can accomplish all of my goals. I am in control of my destiny. If I can envision it, I can make it happen.

♥

I will focus on the good, the positive, the inspiring, and the joyful and avoid the negative.

♥

I love my body, and I look good and feel good.

♥

I trust my instincts when it comes to money-making opportunities.

♥

I am capable of generating unlimited wealth.

♥

I handle my finances with wisdom and make profitable investments.

♥

Every challenge I face is an opportunity for financial growth.

♥

My wealth expands each day as I strive for more.

♥

I am a businesswoman; my success is inevitable.

I am an entrepreneur, and money flows easily to me.

My ideas are innovative and profitable.

I am confident in my ability to make smart decisions and create wealth.

I am successful, and I attract wealth.

I celebrate my financial successes, big or small.

My earning potential is limitless, just like my ambition.

I see abundance everywhere, and I welcome it into my life.

I have overcome so much in my life; nothing can hold me back.

I am manifesting my dreams into financial reality.

I make decisions that are in the best interest of my financial growth.

I am worthy of a prosperous and wealthy life.

I am an embodiment of success and financial freedom.

I create opportunities that earn me a high income.

I am financially savvy, and making money comes naturally to me.

My bank balance is always growing, and I am grateful.

I use my wealth to uplift myself and my community.

I am a radiant beacon of strength and beauty, positively impacting people wherever I go.

Every strand of my hair tells a story of resilience; I proudly carry that history.

I dream big and work daily to make these dreams a beautiful reality.

I can create change, not just for myself but for my community.

I am fearless, and I wear my melanin as a badge of honor.

My voice matters, my thoughts are valuable, and my contributions are significant.

I am deserving of respect, love, and joy simply because I am.

I honor my ancestors and their struggles by shining brightly in today's world.

Every curve, every feature, every part of me is a testament to a rich history and vibrant culture.

I am a force of nature, unstoppable in my pursuit of success and happiness.

I am an amazing gift to myself, my friends, and the world.

I love and appreciate myself. I am who I am, and I love myself.

I do not need the company of others to feel complete. I am more than enough.

The past no longer has control over me. Only the present matters.

Everything I need will appear at the right time and place.

I will not give up on my dreams. It's always too early to give up on my dreams.

I believe in myself and the path I have chosen.

I embrace being positive, and I reject negative thoughts.

I am at peace with my body and accept it as it is.

I am attractive just as I am. I don't need to change anything.

I love and care for my body by exercising, eating healthy, and getting adequate rest.

I am a strong, confident woman who is getting stronger every day.

I laugh, dance, love, and spread joy to all my friends.

I embody strength, carrying myself gracefully through all of life's trials and triumphs.

I am a leader who encourages and values diversity, promoting a culture of inclusivity and respect.

I will always find a way to achieve my goals.

I value kindness, respect, and inclusion.

My blackness is not a limitation but a unique strength that sets me apart.

I am a wellspring of creativity and innovation, continually pushing boundaries and defying expectations.

I refuse to shrink myself for others' comfort. I stand tall and firm in my identity.

I am enough, exactly as I am, and no one's opinion can change that truth.

I pridefully embrace my heritage, drawing strength and inspiration from my roots.

I am the architect of my future, shaping my destiny with determination and courage.

I am beautiful, from the texture of my hair to my skin color.

My potential is limitless, and every day I am reaching new heights.

I fill my mind with positive, empowering thoughts fueling my journey to greatness.

I celebrate my individuality and the unique ways I contribute to the world.

I am a queen, carrying myself with dignity and inspiring others through my journey.

My intelligence guides my decision-making.

The challenges I face make me stronger, wiser, and more resilient.

♥

I take care of my mind, body, and spirit, recognizing that self-care is an act of self-love.

♥

My dreams are valid, my goals are achievable, and I have everything I need to succeed.

♥

I am a phenomenal black woman; I am growing and becoming more fabulous every day.

♥

I appreciate the good in my life while striving for my goals.

♥

I look for ways to use my strengths today.

♥

I live in the moment and make the most of every day.

♥

I seek positive action every day.

♥

I live this day true to my visions of what I want my life to be.

I create change in my life when I need it.

I have everything I need to make today great.

Amazing opportunities are on their way.

I have the power to choose how my day will go.

I stay focused on my vision today.

I look in the mirror and see a proud, beautiful black woman.

I plant seeds today to make my tomorrow better.

I look for moments to go the extra mile today.

I begin the day feeling strong and centered.

Good things are coming my way today.

I focus on high-value activities.
I deserve a love that is pure, honest, and profound.

My life is full of love, and I am ready to share it with someone special.

I start my day grateful for the good that surrounds me.

I am open to new opportunities today.

The only approval I need is my own.

My smile warms the room and draws others towards me.

My actions create constant prosperity.

I am a confident and capable leader.

I easily accept responsibility and make things happen.

My positive attitude influences others and brings good energy to the workplace.

My team trusts me; they have faith in my leadership skills.

My values and integrity are visible in my actions.

I am an innovative leader who inspires my team to think outside the box.

My goals are clear and measurable, and I am dedicated to achieving them.

I lead with empathy and compassion, fostering a culture of kindness and support.

I am an effective communicator, conveying ideas and goals clearly and concisely.

I am resilient in the face of challenges and capable of overcoming them.

I trust my instincts and make confident decisions.

I am a fearless leader who embraces change and takes risks when necessary.

I empower my team to take ownership of their work and take pride in their accomplishments.

I am a visionary leader who inspires my team to achieve great things.

I succeed because of my supportive and motivational beliefs.

I am a strategic thinker who always keeps the big picture in mind.

Every day, I strive to learn something new; I am coachable.

I do not stray from my goals; I move forward and accomplish my goals.

I work with and support my friends, and we achieve our goals together.

I am an empowered woman, ready to conquer any challenge that comes my way.

My value is evident to all who meet me.

I embrace my individuality, and my uniqueness shines through in everything I do.

I permit myself to leave situations that are harmful to me

.Every step I take is leading me toward my ultimate goals and aspirations.

I am proud of the woman I am today and excited for the woman I am becoming.

My mistakes are opportunities for growth and learning.

My potential to succeed is limitless.

I am whole and complete in my solitude and celebrate my independence.

I am a force to be reckoned with.

My body is a beautiful expression of my individuality, strength, and womanhood.

I permit myself to prioritize my happiness and well-being.

Every day, in every way, I am becoming more confident and self-assured.

I love and accept myself unconditionally, knowing that perfection is an illusion.

I respect my emotions and honor my feelings as a part of my unique experience.

My dreams are worthy, my ambition is strong, and my goals are attainable.

I embrace change as a natural part of life and trust my ability to adapt and grow.

I deserve love, respect, and kindness from both myself and others.

I am an embodiment of strength, capable of handling any hurdles that come my way.

I am a fountain of creativity; my ideas are valuable and worth expressing.

♥

I can and will make my dreams a reality.

♥

My life is filled with abundance and gratitude, and I am thankful for every experience.

♥

My voice matters, my opinions are valid, and I express myself with confidence and conviction.

♥

I control my life, and my decisions shape my future.

♥

I respect my journey, appreciate my progress, and look forward to a great future.

♥

My strength is greater than any struggle, and my will is stronger than any obstacle.

♥

I am a fierce, fearless, and fabulous woman, ready to seize every opportunity life brings my way.

♥

Nothing can stand in my way; I am determined and deserve to reach my goals.

I am a beautiful black woman, blessed with beauty, intelligence, kindness, and determination.

My strong will and sense of self will see me through any adversity.

I am deserving of a loving, respectful, and supportive partner.

I am grateful for my family's history and heritage.

I attract healthy, meaningful relationships into my life.

My heart is open and ready for love.

My past relationships do not define me; my future empowers me.

My uniqueness attracts love that is authentic and pure.

I am secure with myself and do not need validation from others.

I am enough, exactly as I am, and the right person will see and value this.

Love finds me effortlessly and naturally.

My love story is unfolding exactly as it should.

I release all past hurts and open myself up to the possibilities of love.

I radiate love, and it attracts the same.

I deserve a love that is as deep and boundless as the love I give.

I am deserving of a partner who celebrates and cherishes me.

I love the glow of beautiful skin.

I trust my journey and the timing of my life.

Every step I take brings me closer to true love.

I am a magnet for love, and I attract love to me.

I am loved for my authenticity and the unique individual that I am.

I deserve a partner who respects, appreciates, and understands me.

I am patient, understanding that true love happens in its own time.

I am surrounded by love in all aspects of my life.

I am attracting a love that reflects the love I have for myself.

The love I seek is also seeking me.

I attract relationships that nourish and fulfill me.

I am open to giving and receiving love healthily and positively.

I embrace the love destined for me, knowing it will come at the right time.

My heart is open and ready to receive love.

I am deserving of a healthy, loving relationship.

I am a magnet for love and positive energy.

I deserve someone who cherishes me for the person I am.

I attract individuals who respect and appreciate my value.

I am attracting a partner who complements my growth and personal evolution.

I am confident in my ability to attract genuine love.

I deserve to be loved fully and unconditionally.

I am attracting a love that is free from manipulation and selfishness.

My inner beauty naturally radiates outwards, attracting authentic love.

I am lovable, and I deserve to feel loved every day.

My past does not dictate my future in love.

I am ready to give and receive love freely and without fear.

My heart is healing and becoming more receptive to love every day.

I am attracting a love that fulfills my emotional and spiritual needs.

I am deserving of respect and kindness, just as I am.

I love myself for who I am, who I am, and who I am becoming.

My presence enriches every room I walk into.

I am embracing my strength, and my vulnerability is a part of it.

I am a powerful creator, capable of manifesting my dreams.

My children are strong, bright, and filled with potential.

My family is a reflection of love, unity, and perseverance.

The love in my family flows in abundance and reaches every member.

I chose to fill my mind with positive thoughts and my body with healthy foods.

I honor the legacy of my ancestors and continue to build a prosperous future for my family.

I will not waste my time worrying about things I cannot control.

I am learning, growing, and becoming a better version of myself daily.

I am valuable, my ideas are helpful, and my contributions are appreciated.

My family thrives on mutual respect, understanding, and unconditional love.

I am more than enough and do not need to prove my worth.

Daily, I pave the way for a brighter future for my family and myself.

I deserve to be where I am and on the best path.

My words, actions, and existence uplift and inspire those around me.

My family's bonds strengthen daily, and we can overcome obstacles together.

I live my life confident in my decision-making.

I am bold, beautiful, and radiant.

I am embracing my uniqueness, which is a source of strength for me.

My family and I are deserving of happiness, success, and love.

My success is a testament to my hard work, resilience, and the strength of my ancestors.

I honor my feelings and understand that they are integral to my journey.

We are a family filled with love, strength, and kindness.

My intelligence and creativity are gifts that I am proud to share with the world.

I am a role model for positivity, and my light shines on my family and community.

Every day I chose to live a life filled with passion and love.

Our family's legacy is one of strength, resilience, and boundless love.

I always carry myself with composure and pride.

I am valuable, and my love is a treasure worth cherishing.

I am worthy of a love that feels like home.

The love I seek is also seeking me.

I let go of past hurts to welcome new love into my life.

I deserve a love that encourages my growth and freedom.

I will not settle for a love that diminishes my worth.

I am worthy of a love that mirrors my deep, radiant love for myself.

I am attracting a partner who honors, respects, cares for, and cherishes me.

I am blessed with my friends and my community.

I laugh every day and thank God for my life.

Everyone I meet can see that I am an intelligent and beautiful black woman.

I am a queen, ruling my world with grace, strength, and wisdom.

My roots are rich, my heritage is powerful, and my future is limitless.

Every obstacle I face is an opportunity for me to demonstrate my resilience.

I embody beauty, strength, and determination in my every breath.

My melanin is the essence of my beauty, radiating from within and glowing throughout.

I am deserving of all the love, joy, and success that life has to offer.

I reject any negative perceptions of myself and embrace the truth of my inherent worthiness.

My voice and opinions are valuable, and I will not be silenced.

I am a beacon of inspiration, guiding others through my actions and achievements.

The challenges I face today are cultivating the wisdom I will share tomorrow.

♥

I am more than enough; I am an abundance of strength, love, and vitality.

♥

I boldly confront adversity, which is no match for my strength and determination.

♥

I lovingly care for myself, nourishing my body, mind, and spirit.

♥

My dreams are valid, achievable, and worth every effort I put toward them.

♥

Every day, in every way, I am becoming more empowered and self-assured.

♥

The energy I bring to the world is transformative and healing.

♥

I confidently claim my space and stand firm in my truth.

♥

My power is an undeniable force, propelling me toward my destiny.

♥

I am an intricate tapestry of strength, courage, and love.

♥

My potential is infinite, my future is bright, and my journey is inspiring.

♥

With every step, I move closer to my dreams, powered by determination and courage.

♥

I release fear, embrace courage, and boldly stride toward my destiny.

♥

My authenticity is my strength, and I honor it by being true to myself.

♥

I respect and honor my body, my vessel for experiencing life's richness.

♥

I am a phenomenal woman, resilient, strong, and boundlessly capable.

♥

I can do it all, and I am competent.

Thank You

Hello, I hope you have enjoyed this book. I would love to hear your thoughts on this book.

Many readers are unaware of how difficult it is to get reviews and how much they help authors like me.
I would greatly appreciate it if you could support me and help get the word out to other people about this book.

It is easy to leave a review; please click on the link below or scan the QR code with your phone. I am very grateful for your support.

https://amzn.to/3uzyi5d

References

Balanced Black Girl. (n.d.). 10 affirmations guide glow up. Retrieved June 29, 2023, from https://www.balancedblackgirl.com/10-affirmations-guide-glow-up/

Gratefulness.Me. (2023). 20 Positive Affirmations to Improve Your Body Image. Retrieved from https://blog.gratefulness.me/20-positive-affirmations-to-improve-your-body-image/

Gregg, S. (2021, May). A guide to affirmations and how to use them. Psychology Today. Retrieved June 29, 2023, from https://www.psychologytoday.com/us/blog/click-here-happiness/202105/guide-affirmations-and-how-use-them

Happier Human. (n.d.). Positive affirmations for women. Retrieved June 29, 2023, from https://www.happierhuman.com/positive-affirmations-women/

Happier Human. (n.d.). Leadership Affirmations. Retrieved June 29, 2023, from https://www.happierhuman.com/leadership-affirmations/

Let's Learn Slang. (n.d.). Positive Affirmations for Black Women. Retrieved June 29, 2023, from https://letslearnslang.com/positive-affirmations-for-black-women/

Live Bold and Bloom. (n.d.). Positive Affirmations for Women. Retrieved June 29, 2023, from https://liveboldandbloom.com/09/self-confidence/positive-affirmations-women

Our West Nest. (2021, September 3). Empowering Affirmations for Black Women. Our West Nest. https://www.ourwestnest.com/blogposts/2020/11/30/morning-affirmations-and-quotes-for-black-women-to-empower-themselves)

Our West Nest. (2020, November 30). Morning affirmations and quotes for blackwomen to empower themselves. Retrieved June 29, 2023, from https://www.ourwestnest.com/blogposts/2020/11/30/morning-affirmations-and-quotes-for-black-women-to-empower-themselves

Our West Nest. (2020, November 30). Morning affirmations and quotes for blackwomen to empower themselves. Retrieved June 29, 2023,

from https://www.ourwestnest.com/blogposts/2020/11/30/morning-affirmations-an
d-quotes-for-black-women-to-empower-themselves

Positive Affirmations Center. (n.d.). Positive Affirmations for Leaders. Retrieved June
29, 2023, from https://positiveaffirmationscenter.com/positive-affirmations-for-leaders/

Positive Affirmationsly. (n.d.). Positive Affirmations for Black Women. Retrieved June
29, 2023, from https://positiveaffirmationsly.com/positive-affirmations-black-women/

Psychology Today. (2023). A Guide to Affirmations and How to Use Them. Psychology Today.
   https://www.psychologytoday.com/us/blog/click-here-happiness/202105/guide-affi
rmations-and-how-use-them

Sager, J. (n.d.). Money Affirmations. Parade. Retrieved June 29, 2023, from https://
parade.com/1350894/jessicasager/money-affirmations/

Self Inc. (2023). 7 Money Affirmations to Attract Financial Abundance. Retrieved
from https://www.self.inc/blog/money-affirmations

Self Inc. (2023). Money Affirmations. Retrieved from https://www.self.inc/blog/m
oney-affirmations

She Made By Grace. (n.d.). Affirmations for Black Women. Retrieved June 29, 2023,
from https://shemadebygrace.com/affirmations-for-black-women/

Take The Lead Women. (2023). 6 Affirmations for Black Women Leaders in the
Workplace. Retrieved from https://www.taketheleadwomen.com/blog/6-affirmations
-black-women-leaders-workplace/

The Good Positive. (n.d.). Positive Affirmations for Leaders. Retrieved June 29, 2023,
from https://thegoodpositive.com/positive-affirmations-for-leaders/

Unfinished Success. (n.d.). Affirmations for Black Women. Retrieved June 29, 2023,
from https://unfinishedsuccess.com/affirmations-for-black-women/

Verywell Mind. (n.d.). Positive Daily Affirmations. Retrieved June 29, 2023, from
https://www.verywellmind.com/positive-daily-affirmations-709706

Wealthy Woman Finance. (2023). 150 Positive Affirmations For Success and Wealth
(in 2023). Retrieved June 29, 2023

Made in United States
Orlando, FL
15 December 2024

55801720R00075